The Saints

21 Models for Good Living

Reproducible Handouts for Primary Grades

Francine M. O'Connor

Active Learning for Catholic Kids

Hi-Time✳Pflaum

Dayton, OH

The Saints

21 Models for Good Living

Reproducible Handouts for Primary Grades

Francine M. O'Connor

Cover and interior design by Larissa Qvick

The Scripture quotations contained herein are from the *New Revised Standard Version of the Bible:* Catholic Edition, ©1993 and 1989 by the Division of Christian Education of the National Council of the Churches of Christ in the U.S.A. All rights reserved. Used by permission.

©2000 Hi-Time*Pflaum, Dayton, OH 45449. All rights reserved. Photocopying of the material herein is permitted by the publisher for noncommercial use. The permission line must appear on each reproduced page. Any other type of reproduction, transmittal, storage, or retrieval, in any form or by any means, whether electronic or mechanical, including recording, is not permitted without the written consent of the publisher.

ISBN: 0-937997-52-8

Contents

Mary, Mother of God (first century)

Name_____

Feast: January 1
A Surprise Announcement

An angel came to visit Mary one day and told her she was to be the mother of God's son. What a wonderful surprise for Mary! Every year we celebrate that wonderful day when God's son was born to Mary. Solve this rebus puzzle and find the name of that most happy day.

P + 🪑 + L - 🪣 + 💍 - R

+ OATS - 🐐 - N + T + 🎭 - K =

Answer: _ _ _ _ _ _ _ _

St. John Bosco

(1815-1888)

Name_____

Feast: January 31
Caring for God's Children

Father John Bosco spent all of his grown-up life taking care of homeless boys. He and his mother opened a home for them and lived there with them. He cared for them with lots of love and encouragement. He paid for all their needs by preaching, writing, and collecting donations. He recruited others to help him. They became known as the Society of St. Francis de Sales (the Salesians). He also started an Order of sisters to take care of poor and neglected girls. He was especially interested in teaching young people how they could earn a living. Solve the acrostic to discover what John Bosco is called.

__	__	__	__	__
7	18	9	4	11

__	__	__
13	2	6

__	__	__	__
3	15	14	7

__	__	__
17	5	1

__	__	__	__	__
15	10	9	5	6

__	__	__	__
7	12	16	1

__	__	__	__
18	8	9	4

__ __ __ __ __ __   __ __ __ __ __   __ __   __ __ __ __ __ .
1 2 3 4 5 6   7 8 9 10 11   12 13   14 15 16 17 18

St. Paul Miki and Companions (died: 1597)

Name_____

Feast: February 6
Missionaries in Japan

St. Paul Miki was a Japanese Jesuit brother and a wonderful preacher. Many who listened to Paul and his fellow missionaries learned to love Jesus with all their hearts. More and more people began to follow what Paul and his companions taught them about Jesus. But the Japanese ruler of that time didn't want the people to worship Jesus. So he condemned Paul, nine other priests, and seventeen laypeople to die on crosses. Paul Miki forgave those who killed him, as Jesus had done. But even after they were crucified, their work did not die. Many who believed in Jesus through their teachings worshiped Jesus secretly for many, many years.

Using the words in the Word List below, fill in the blanks.

1.   Paul Miki was a __ __ __ __ __ __ __ __ .

2.   He talked about Jesus to the people of __ __ __ __ __.

3.   The leaders of the country did not want the people to worship __ __ __ __ __.

4.   Paul Miki and the others were __ __ __ __ __ __ __ __ __.

5.   Christians in Japan continued to __ __ __ __ __ __ __ Jesus in secret.

6.   Paul Miki teaches us how to __ __ __ __ __ __ __.

Word List

crucified   Jesus   Japan   preacher   forgive   worship

Has anyone done something to you that really made you sad? Will you try to forgive that person in your heart?

St. Valentine

(died: 269)

Name_____

Feast: February 14
Love Notes

St. Valentine was a bishop who believed in love. He was put into prison during the Roman persecution of the Christians. From prison, he sent notes of encouragement to his people. He told them to be loyal to Jesus and to love God and others. These were the first Valentines.

Cut out the large heart pattern and trace around it onto red construction paper. Cut out the large red heart and paste it onto a white paper doily. Then cut out the smaller white heart, color the message with bright markers and paste it into the center of your red heart.

St. Patrick

(389-461)

Name_____

Feast: March 17
Patrick and the Shamrock

St. Patrick was a missionary who traveled to Ireland to teach the people there about God. Patrick used a small, three-leafed plant called the shamrock, or three-leaf clover, to teach the people something that is very important about God but also hard to understand. Can you guess what that important mystery is?

Solve the rebus to find the answer. Then you can color the shamrock green and paste or write the three names from the Word List onto the three leaves of the shamrock.

Word List

**God the Father
Jesus the Son
The Holy Spirit**

- PACK + B + | + L - ⬤ + T + Y =

_____

Answer: __ __ __ __ __ __ __ __

St. Joseph

(first century)

Name_____

Feast: March 19

A Secret Message

Joseph, the husband of Mary, had an angel visit him in a dream (see Matthew 1:20-21). You can find out what the angel told Joseph by solving this puzzle.

Starting at the arrow, write down every other letter to find out what the angel told Joseph. (You will use all the letters to get the answer.)

____ ____ ____ _ ___ ___ ____

___ __ ____ ___ _____.

Something Extra

Saints are busy people. They work hard. Some, like St. Joseph, work to support their families. This is God's way of telling us that honest work brings us closer to God. From the clues on this page, can you tell what work St. Joseph did? Write it on the line.

St. Joseph was a _____.

St. Bernadette

(1844-1879)

Name_____

Feast: April 16

The Message of Lourdes

One hundred and fifty years ago, Mary appeared to a young girl named Bernadette, who came from a very poor French family. For two weeks, Mary appeared every day to Bernadette. Then one day Mary told Bernadette to wash in the water from the spring—but there was no spring there. So Mary told Bernadette where to dig, and Bernadette dug in the dry ground until water started to bubble up! The water from this same spring continues to bubble up even today and many pilgrims go to that spring hoping to be healed of their illnesses. This all happened in Lourdes, France, and a famous shrine is there today, dedicated to Our Lady of Lourdes.

When Our Lady instructed Bernadette to wash in a spring that was not there, Bernadette obeyed. Even though she did not see a spring, she knew there must be one if Our Lady said so. Solve this rebus to learn something special that Bernadette shares with the people who come to Lourdes for healing.

F +  - N - T +  - ⑩ - K + H =

_____

Answer: ___ ___ ___ ___ ___ ___ ___

St. Brendan

(484-577)

Name_____

Feast Day: May 16
The Sailor Saint

St. Brendan was a missionary who lived in Ireland. He made many journeys to spread the Good News of Jesus. He was most famous for one journey that took seven years. He and his crew sailed across the ocean. Some stories say they reached North America. Because of his many ocean journeys, St. Brendan became the patron saint of sailors.

Here is a maze of St. Brendan's voyage. Can you help the little boat find its way from Ireland to North America?

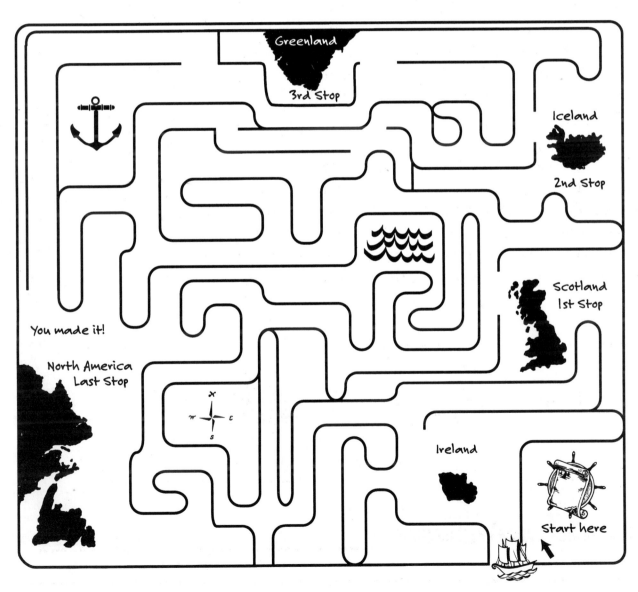

St. Joan of Arc

(1412-1431)

Name_____

Feast: May 30
Maid of Orleans

St. Joan of Arc was a young girl from Orleans, France. She heard the voices of saints calling on her to save her country, which was at war with England. In those days, women didn't go off to fight in wars, but Joan put on a suit of armor and became the leader of the army! She fought and won many battles, but in the end she was arrested by her enemies and burned at the stake. Joan was very brave and not afraid to do what God and the saints had called her to do. Today she is the patron saint of France.

TIC, TAC, TOE

See if you can find three identical pictures. Hint: the identical pictures will all be in a row—across, up and down, or diagonal as in Tic, Tac, Toe. When you have found them, you may color all the pictures.

Remember to color the three identical pictures exactly alike. Make all the others as different as you can.

For your eyes only

Have you ever been asked to do something you knew you should do, but didn't want to do? Were you like St. Joan?

Could you be more like St. Joan in the future?

St. Charles Lwanga (died: 1886)

Name_____

Feast: June 3
Martyrs of Uganda

Once, in Uganda, which is in Africa, there was a very cruel king. Charles Lwanga, a Christian, was one of the king's pages, who is a kind of helper to the king. When Charles Lwanga warned the king to change his sinful ways, the king became angry. He hated all who believed in Jesus. He ordered Charles and fourteen other Christian pages burned to death. Because Charles Lwanga had the courage to speak up for what is right, he lost his life—and became a saint. There is a song called "This Little Light of Mine." The song tells about letting Jesus' light shine through us. Charles Lwanga let his light shine for all his people. Follow these easy directions to make a Gospel Light of your own. Then let your light shine for all to see.

Cut the candle holder from black construction paper, the candle from your favorite color and the flame from two colors—yellow on the outside, red in the center. Now color and cut out Jesus' message. Paste everything together as shown on a larger piece of colored construction paper.

SAMPLE

Let your light shine for all the world to see.

ℒET YOUR LIGHT SHINE
FOR ALL THE WORLD TO SEE.

Bl. Kateri Tekakwitha

Name_____

(1656-1680)

Feast: July 14
Lily of the Mohawks

Kateri Tekakwitha was a Native American from the Mohawk tribe. When she was very young, her parents died of a sickness that left Kateri scarred and almost blind. She learned about Jesus and became a Christian. Some members of her village did not believe in Jesus and they sent her away.

Kateri left her people and went to live with a Christian tribe in Canada, where a kind priest helped her to prepare for her First Communion. She devoted the rest of her life to spreading God's love among her people.

Fill in the blanks using the words in the Word List below.

1. Kateri Tekakwitha belonged to the __ __ __ __ __ __ tribe.

2. Kateri learned about Jesus and became a __ __ __ __ __ __ __ __ __.

3. Kateri left her village and traveled to __ __ __ __ __ __.

4. She made her __ __ __ __ __   __ __ __ __ __ __ __ __ __ in Canada.

Word List

Christian   Mohawk   Canada   First Communion

Make a Home Like Kateri's

Kateri lived in a home made of wood and bark. This kind of home is called a tepee. Using the pattern given on the separate page, make a tepee to remind you of Kateri. Color the tepee, which is decorated with drawings of God's gifts to us.

Then cut on the dotted line, roll the page together so that the dots and triangles meet. Paste or tape the ends together so the tepee stands upright. Place it where you can see it every morning. Then, like Kateri, you will begin each day remembering the love and the goodness of God.

fold

St. John the Baptist (died: c 30)

Name_____

Feast: August 29
Preparing for Jesus

When the angel told Mary her happy secret about being the mother of Jesus, he also told her another secret. Mary's cousin Elizabeth was also going to have a remarkable son. Elizabeth's son was named John. God chose John to tell the whole world that Jesus was coming to save them from their sins. John warned the people to change their evil ways and turn back to God.

John lived in the desert, ate strange food, and wore strange, rough clothes. Here are some of the things John wore. Cut out the figure of John on the second page and trace around it on poster board or card board. Cut the figure out. Then cut each piece of clothing and trace it onto construction paper. Be careful not to cut the tabs off. Now cut the clothes out of the construction paper and dress John in his desert outfit.

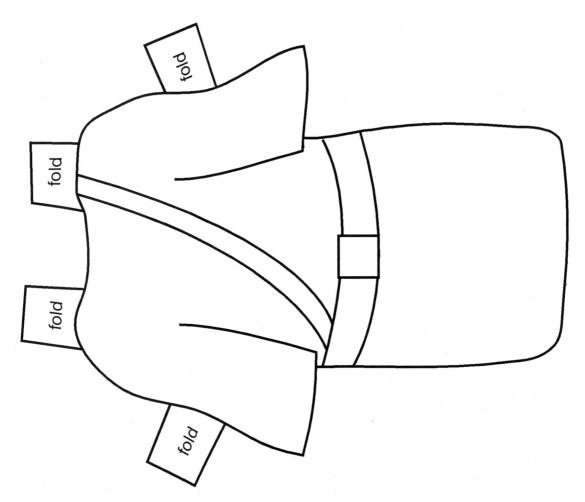

fold

fold

fold

fold

Bl. Jeanne Jugan

(1792-1879)

Name_____

Feast: August 30
Helping the Poor

Have you ever won an award? People win awards for all sorts of things. There are sports trophies, blue ribbons for spelling bees, medals for bravery, silver cups for bowling, and certificates for good work. Jeanne Jugan was given an award for her work in helping the poor. Jeanne and two friends started a religious order of women to work with the poor. If you can solve the acrostic, you will learn the very fitting name given to these women.

Write the answers to the picture clues in the blanks, then put the letters over their matching numbers in the answer. If you don't know an answer, go on to the next one and then come back. Many letters are repeated and will give you clues to the answers you don't know.

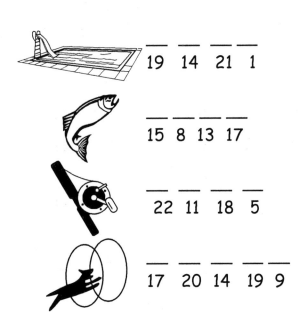

___ ___ ___ ___
19 14 21 1

___ ___ ___ ___
15 8 13 17

___ ___ ___ ___
22 11 18 5

___ ___ ___ ___ ___
17 20 14 19 9

___ ___ ___ ___
3 6 7 16

___ ___ ___ ___
15 2 12 6

___ ___ ___ ___
1 8 9 4

___ ___ ___ ___
10 2 22 6

___ ___ ___ ___ ___ ___ ___ ___ ___ ___ ___ ___ ___
1 2 3 4 5 6   7 8 9 10 11 12 13

___ ___ ___ ___ ___ ___ ___ ___ ___ ___
14 15   16 17 18   19 20 21 22

St. Vincent de Paul (1580-1660)

Name_____

Feast: September 27
Patron Saint of Charity

Vincent de Paul was the son of French peasants. He went to college and became a priest. Once, when he was traveling, he was captured and sold as a slave in Algeria. It was two years before he could escape. Vincent spent the rest of his life working for the poor. He built hospitals and orphanages and he ransomed Christian slaves in Africa. Today, St.

Vincent de Paul Societies around the world still work to help the poor.

Hidden in this square are items you can give to your local St. Vincent de Paul Society or to another organization that helps the poor. See how many items you find hidden in this square.

BLANKETS	CLOTHING	DIAPERS	FOOD	MONEY
SHEETS	SHOES	SOAP	TOOTHPASTE	TOWELS

```
S  H  E  E  T  S  A  E  B  T
H  D  I  A  P  E  R  S  F  O
M  O  N  E  Y  M  C  I  K  O
E  O  X  P  V  Q  L  M  T  T
S  W  I  X  F  O  O  D  O  H
B  L  A  N  K  E  T  S  W  P
U  Y  H  C  F  Z  H  T  E  A
N  S  H  O  E  S  I  O  L  S
J  R  N  E  B  S  N  L  S  T
C  G  S  O  A  P  G  H  D  E
```

Is there a St. Vincent de Paul Society in your parish or diocese? If so, try to find out the things they do to help people.

St. Jerome

(340-400)

Name_____

Feast Day: September 30
Translator of God's Word

God speaks to us through the Scriptures — the stories and lessons about God and Jesus that we find in the Bible. The Bible tells us how to know God better and understand what God expects of us.

St. Jerome lived a long, long time ago. He wanted all the people in the world to know God's love. The Bible was written in a language most people didn't know, so Jerome spent most of his life translating the Bible into the language that people would be able to read.

Because of all his hard work for God, St. Jerome earned a special title in the Church. Solve the code below to learn St. Jerome's special title.

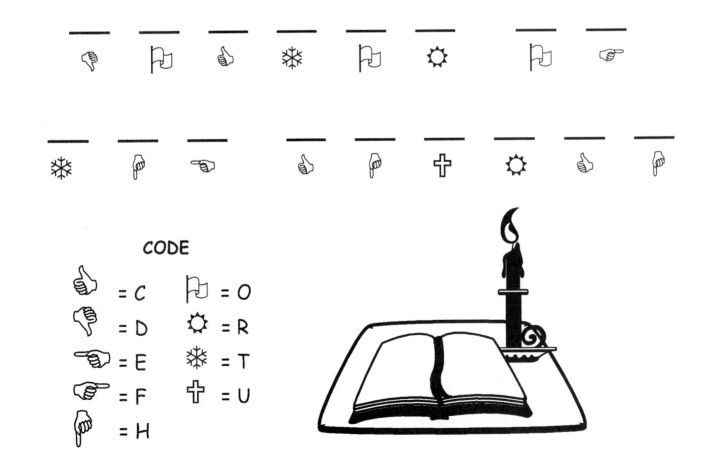

CODE

👍 = C   🏳 = O

👎 = D   ☼ = R

☞ = E   ❄ = T

☞ = F   ✝ = U

👇 = H

St. Thérèse of Lisieux (1873-1897)

Name_____

Feast: October 1
Saint of the Little Way

When Thérèse was only four years old, her mother died. Thérèse was raised by her older sisters, and followed their examples by becoming a Carmelite nun. Thérèse really always wanted to be a missionary and to do grand and wonderful things for God. When this didn't happen, she decided she would do every little thing she could for God—every little chore would be her prayer, her gift to God. She called it her "little way to Jesus." Besides being known as the Little Flower, St. Thérèse has also been called the "saint of the little way."

You, too, can do "little things for God" each day just as Thérèse did. Here is a good way to remind yourself each day this week to do something for God. Make a prayer chain by coloring these "Little Prayer-and-Action Strips" in whatever colors you choose. Cut out the strips, and connect them to make the chain. Hang the chain near your bed. Each morning, carefully remove one strip, say the prayer, and follow the day's directions.

 Sunday: St. Thérèse, help me to smile at everyone I meet today.

 Monday: St. Thérèse, I will do one extra chore today in Jesus' name.

 Tuesday: St. Thérèse, today I will plant a seed to thank God for the wonders of our world.

 Wednesday: St. Thérèse, on this day I will draw a picture for someone who is lonely or sad.

 Thursday: St. Thérèse, I will thank my teacher today for helping my mind to grow.

 Friday: St. Thérèse, today I will be good to someone who is younger than I am.

 Saturday: St. Thérèse, today I will say an extra prayer for those who take care of me every day.

St. Francis of Assisi (1182-1226)

Name_____

Feast: October 4
Bless All Creatures

St. Francis was a gentle saint who cared for all of God's creatures. On St. Francis's feast day, many churches have a blessing for pets because of Francis's love for animals and birds.

You can make a St. Francis Blessing Card for your pet or for any animal you like. Fold the page in half from top to bottom, then again in from side to side. Cut out the square on the dotted lines as marked on the front of the card.

Then paste your pet's picture or a picture of your favorite animal in the frame. (Use magazines to find a picture you like if you don't have a photograph.) Color the picture of St. Francis, sign your name on the back of the card, and your blessing card is ready to display where you can read it often.

This Blessing Card
made by

O gentle St. Francis,
you were always kind to all
of God's creatures.

Watch over and protect
all animals, birds, fish,
and every other creature in
the world.

Help me and all people
to always respect these
wonderful gifts from God.

St. Martin de Porres (1579-1639)

Name_____

Feast: November 3
A Kind and Gentle Man

Martin de Porres cared for all who could not care for themselves—the sick, the slaves from Africa, the Indians of Peru, even the tiniest animals. There are many stories about this gentle saint. Some are true and some are legends. But they all tell us of Martin's love and kindness. In one story, Martin promises the mice in the monastery kitchen that he will feed them if they will move to the garden. The mice left the kitchen, Martin kept his promise, and the cook was never bothered by mice again.

MARTIN'S A-MAZE-ING MOUSE MAZE
Can you help the mice find their way from the kitchen to the garden? St. Martin is waiting there to feed them, but they must get past the cook with his broom, the cat with her hungry eyes, and the hidden mouse trap.

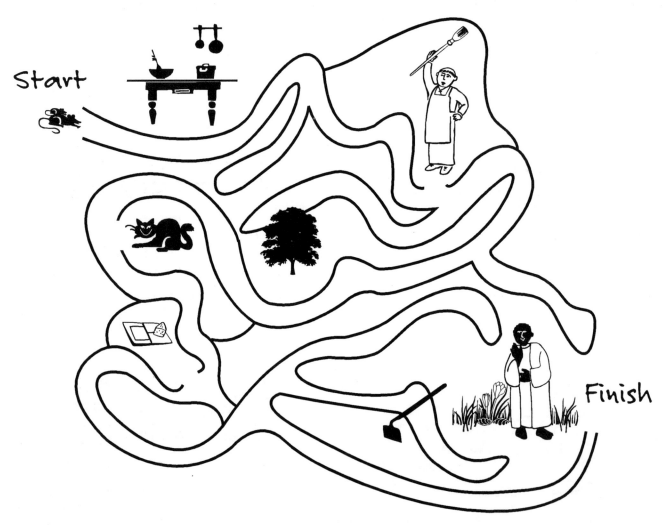

Start

Finish

St. Elizabeth of Hungary

(1207-1231)

Name_____

Feast: November 17

A Bouquet of Cheer

St. Elizabeth lived in a wonderful castle with her husband and four children. She was a kind and generous woman who loved God's people. She built a hospital at the foot of her castle to care for the sick. When her husband died, she was sent away, but she continued to work for those who were sick. After she died, many miracles of healing were reported by those who asked for her prayers.

You can make a bouquet of cheer for someone you know who is sick or lonely. Using carbon paper, trace the patterns on this page onto brightly colored construction paper. Make one center (circle) and five petals for each blossom. Paste your finished blossoms onto a large sheet of construction paper, give them pipe-cleaner stems. Color the cheery words and paste them on your bouquet.

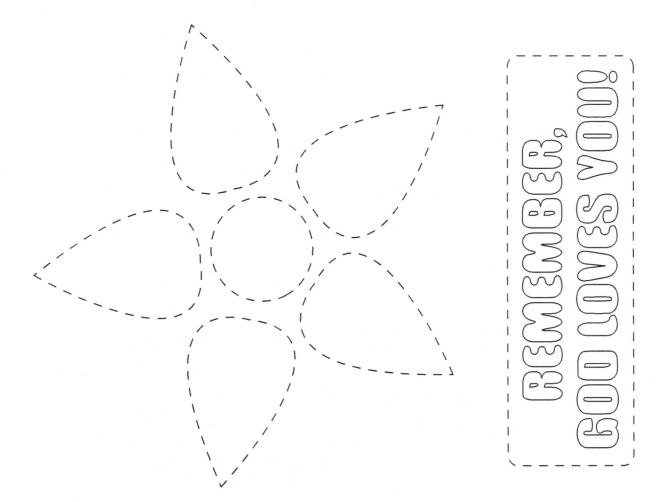

REMEMBER, GOD LOVES YOU!

St. Nicholas

(fourth century)

Feast: December 6
The Spirit of Christmas

St. Nicholas was a bishop who lived a long time ago. There are many legends about Nicholas. One story tells how he threw three bags of gold into the house of a very poor man who had three daughters. Nicholas wanted to make sure the three girls would be taken care of. In some countries, children exchange gifts on St. Nicholas' feast day, just as we do at Christmas.

Make a St. Nicholas Day promise card to celebrate this generous saint. Fold a piece of construction paper in thirds. Cut out the bag of gold pattern and trace it onto the construction paper, making sure that the sides of the bag touch the folded sides of the paper. Cut away the paper from the top and bottom of the bag pattern, but be careful not to cut through the folds. (When you unfold the paper, you should have three bags in a row.) Color, cut out, and paste the bishop's miter to the front of the first bag. Inside, on each bag, write one of the words below and add your own promise. (For example, for Justice, you can promise to always play fair; for Charity, to share your toys; for Love of God, to pray every day.)

Justice   Charity   Love of God

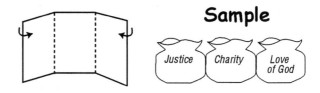

Sample

Justice   Charity   Love of God

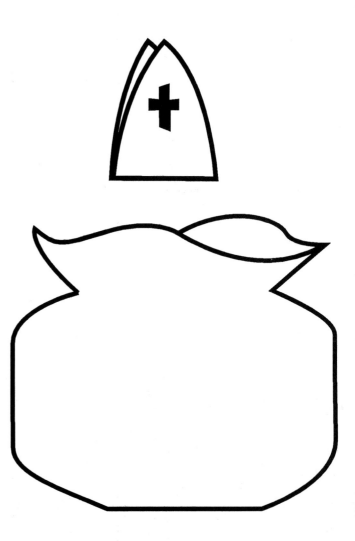

Bl. Juan Diego

(1474-1548)

Name_____

Feast: December 9
The Beautiful Lady

Did you ever think that God and the saints can't see you, or that you are not famous enough to become a saint yourself? The story of Juan Diego, a simple Mexican peasant who became part of a miracle, is a sign of how closely God watches over each of us, no matter how rich or important we are. On his way to town, Juan saw a beautiful lady on a hill. The lady sent Juan with a message to the bishop. The bishop did not believe Juan. He asked Juan for proof. The lady gave him proof—for on that spot, roses were

growing in the middle of winter! The people never forgot this wonderful miracle. By coming to Juan and his people, the lady was telling them that God loves them and cares about them. Today a great church stands where roses once bloomed in the snow.

Here is a "flowery" puzzle for you to do. Match the flowers to the correct letters below, and you will find the name of the beautiful lady.

Code

🌸 =A   =G   ✿ = R

=D   =L   ✛ = U

=E   = O   =Y

=F   = P

___ ___ ___   ___ ___ ___ ___   ___ ___

___ ___ ___ ___ ___ ___ ___ ___ ___.

Notes to Teacher

Mary, Mother of God: A Surprise Announcement
P + [CHAIR] + L - [PAIL] + [RING] -R + [OATS] -
[GOAT] - N + T + [MASK] - K = CHRISTMAS

St. John Bosco: Caring for God's Children
Clues: shirt; fan; toys; top; onion; soup; hair
Answer: Patron saint of youth.

St. Patrick: Patrick and the Shamrock
[PATRICK] - [PACK] + B + [NAIL] + L - [BALL] + T
+ Y = TRINITY

St. Joseph: A Secret Message
Mary will have a son and you are to name him Jesus.

St. Bernadette: The Message of Lourdes
F + [ANT] - N - T + [KITTEN] - [10] - K + H = FAITH

St. Brendan: The Sailor Saint

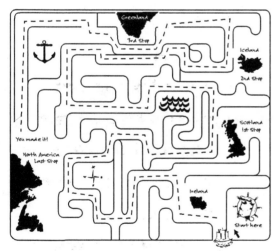

Bl. Jeanne Jugan: Helping the Poor
Picture Clues: pool; fish; reel; hoops; test; fire; list;
tire
Answer: Little Sisters of the Poor

St. Vincent De Paul: Patron Saint of Charity

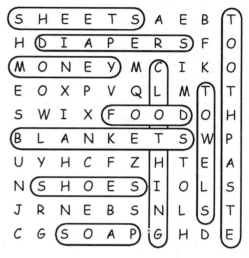

St. Jerome: Translator of God's Word
Answer: Doctor of the Church

St. Francis of Assisi
Folding Instructions: When photocopying this activity,
you can copy the directions on one side of a sheet of
paper and the artwork on the other side. If you do
this, remind the children to fold the page so that the
directions end up on the inside.

St. Martin de Porres: A Kind and Gentle Man

Bl. Juan Diego: The Beautiful Lady
Answer: Our Lady of Guadalupe